Ash's Garden

Ash's Garden

Joseph Coelho
Monique Steele

Collins

PUMPKIN
courgette

Contents

Chapter 1 2
Make a bug hotel 12
Chapter 2 14
Pond wildlife 24
Chapter 3 26
Garden design 34
Chapter 4 36
Storm Bertha 46
Chapter 5 48
Vegetable patch 56
Chapter 6 58
Mayfly life cycle 68
About the author 70
About the illustrator 72
Book chat 74

Chapter 1

Ash's garden is seriously dull. It's all fake grass and lifeless, and when the sky is grey it's even worse. The birds fly over his garden – they never stop to visit. There are no flowers and so no bees. The earth is covered in plastic grass and so there are no worms.

Ash used to go out in the garden to explore on warm days, but nothing grows out there so there's not much to look at. From the doorway he can see every corner. He can see the edge of the fake grass touch every fence panel. There are no mysteries, no hidden parts, nothing to be discovered.

Then one day Ash discovers a book.
It's a sort of guidebook full of pictures,
and it shows him how to bring wildlife
back to a garden. His grandma calls it
WILD LIFE, smiling as she tickles him.

Ash shares the book with his grandma. Grandma doesn't have much experience of gardening. The gardening was always done by Ash's grandpa. But Grandma starts to flick through Ash's book.
She sees the WILD LIFE almost springing up off the page! Then, something inside her blossoms. Together, Ash and Grandma decide to make a change.

Ash grabs one end of the plastic grass. It is a huge sheet that smothers the ground. Grandma goes to the other side and together they start to roll and roll and roll the fake grass up.

Grandma asked a local builder to put the plastic grass down after Grandpa passed away. Maybe they didn't do it right, it is old now and comes up easily. Underneath is soil. Dark crumbly soil.

Ash gets an idea from the book: making raised beds. These are like gigantic pots for plants with deep roots.

Bertie from next door notices them working. "What are you doing?" asks Bertie.

"We're making a garden," says Ash. "We just need some materials to make a raised bed."

Bertie smiles. "I have just the thing," he says. He gives Grandma some old planks and wooden poles called stakes. Together Bertie, Grandma and Ash hammer the stakes into the soil and screw the planks in place. A large, raised bed now sits in the garden!

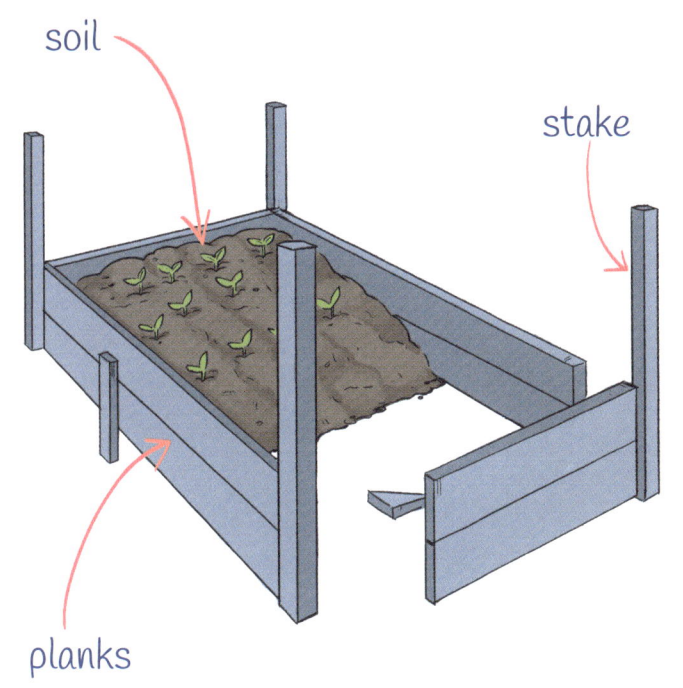

soil

stake

planks

They fill the raised bed up with soil, poke holes with their fingers and plant seeds. Ash uses an old plastic bottle as a watering can and waters the seeds.

"I can't wait to see what flowers we get!" says Ash.

"Neither can I," says Grandma.

There is a hole in the ground where they took out the soil to fill the raised bed. "That would make a great pond!" says Bertie.

Ash flicks through his guidebook and reads out the instructions for a pond.

A pond where frogs can leap and newts can swim and dragonflies can hover. Bertie, Grandma and Ash feel their hearts burst with joy like waterlilies opening.

Grandma seizes a spade and makes the hole for the pond even bigger. Ash and Bertie take out stones, making the soil nice and smooth.

Together they go to the local garden centre and get sand and a pond liner. There they see their neighbour Esmerelda. "What are you doing?" she asks.

"We're adding a pond to our garden," says Ash hopping up and down with excitement just like a frog.

"I have just the thing for that," says Esmerelda. "I'll pop round later today."

Make a bug hotel

- Take a clean old tin.
- Pack it full of sticks, pine cones, leaves and twigs.
- Put it in a quiet spot.
- See how many insects move in!

twig

pine cone

tin

hollow stick

13

Chapter 2

Back at the garden, Ash and Grandma put sand down in the hole to make a nice smooth base for the pond liner. Meanwhile Bertie makes some tea.

"This is thirsty work, I'm exhausted!" says Bertie. "But at least I found some cookies."

They chomp on cookies and get ready to lay the pond liner.

The pond liner is a huge sheet of thick plastic that makes the pond watertight. Together, they spread it over the hole and smooth out all the creases.

Esmerelda arrives with some large stones from her garden. "You can use these to put around the edge of your pond," she says. "They'll also make a brilliant ramp for wildlife like frogs and newts to get in and out."

The stones are big, round and beautiful. "Thanks so much," says Ash, as he places the stones all around the edge to make a gentle slope for creatures to climb.

stones

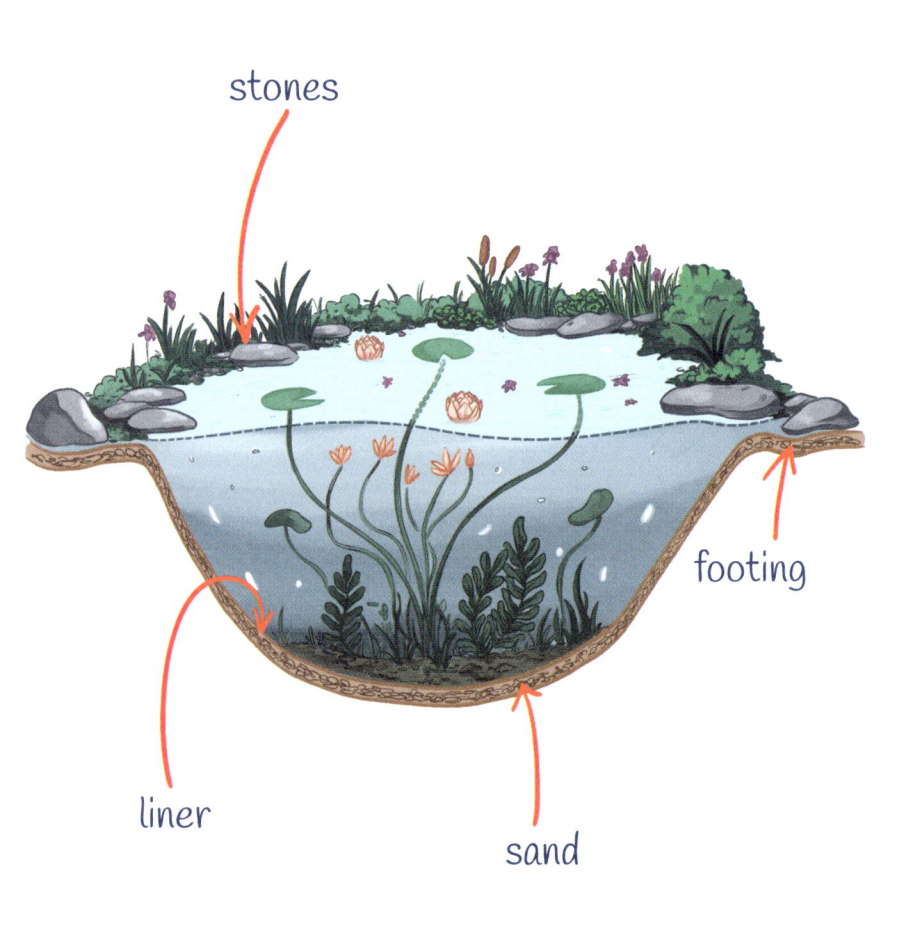

footing

liner

sand

"All we need now is water and our pond will be complete," says Grandma.

Ash looks in his gardening guidebook. "It says here we should use rainwater, but it hasn't rained in ages," he says.

Ash, Bertie, Grandma and Esmeralda look up at the sky ... there's not a single cloud. "We'll have to wait, I'm afraid," says Grandma.

Ash waits, and waits, and waits. Days pass without a single drop of rain. But the waiting is OK, because Ash and Grandma visit some local gardens for inspiration.

They see fruit trees getting ready to bud. They see tree ferns with their coiled leaves preparing to burst forth. They see bug hotels – empty but ready to buzz with insect guests! Ash makes lots of notes in his notebook, just as his guidebook advises. He also draws lots of pictures to help him remember what he's seen.

That night it rains for hours, but when Ash wakes in the morning the pond is still not full. Ash's heart sinks.

But guess what? Word has got round about their pond and before long, there is a knock at the door.

All Ash's neighbours are lined up along the street! They are all carrying watering cans which they've filled up from their water butts. Some of them also have buckets and even plant pots from their gardens, brimming with rainwater from the previous night.

The neighbours make their way through the house. "Careful – don't spill any!" laughs Grandma.

Out in the garden, they empty their watering cans, buckets and rain-filled plant pots into the pond. In no time at all, it is full.

Ash dives into his book. It says that ponds need to be left alone once they are full, to allow wildlife to settle in.

"Can't we add some frogs and newts from a neighbour's pond?" asks Grandma.

"NO!" says Ash. "It says here that doing that can spread disease from pond to pond. We should wait for any wildlife to find the pond naturally. Adding water plants can help, though."

Grandma and Ash go back to
the garden centre and pick out some
dark green hornwort and water moss
to give oxygen to the water, and
some waterlilies and irises for their
bright colours. "It's like we're decorating
a home for our guests – the frogs and
newts," says Ash.

"I hope they don't take too long to move
in," says Grandma.

hornwort

water moss

water lilies

smooth newt

common frog

Pond wildlife

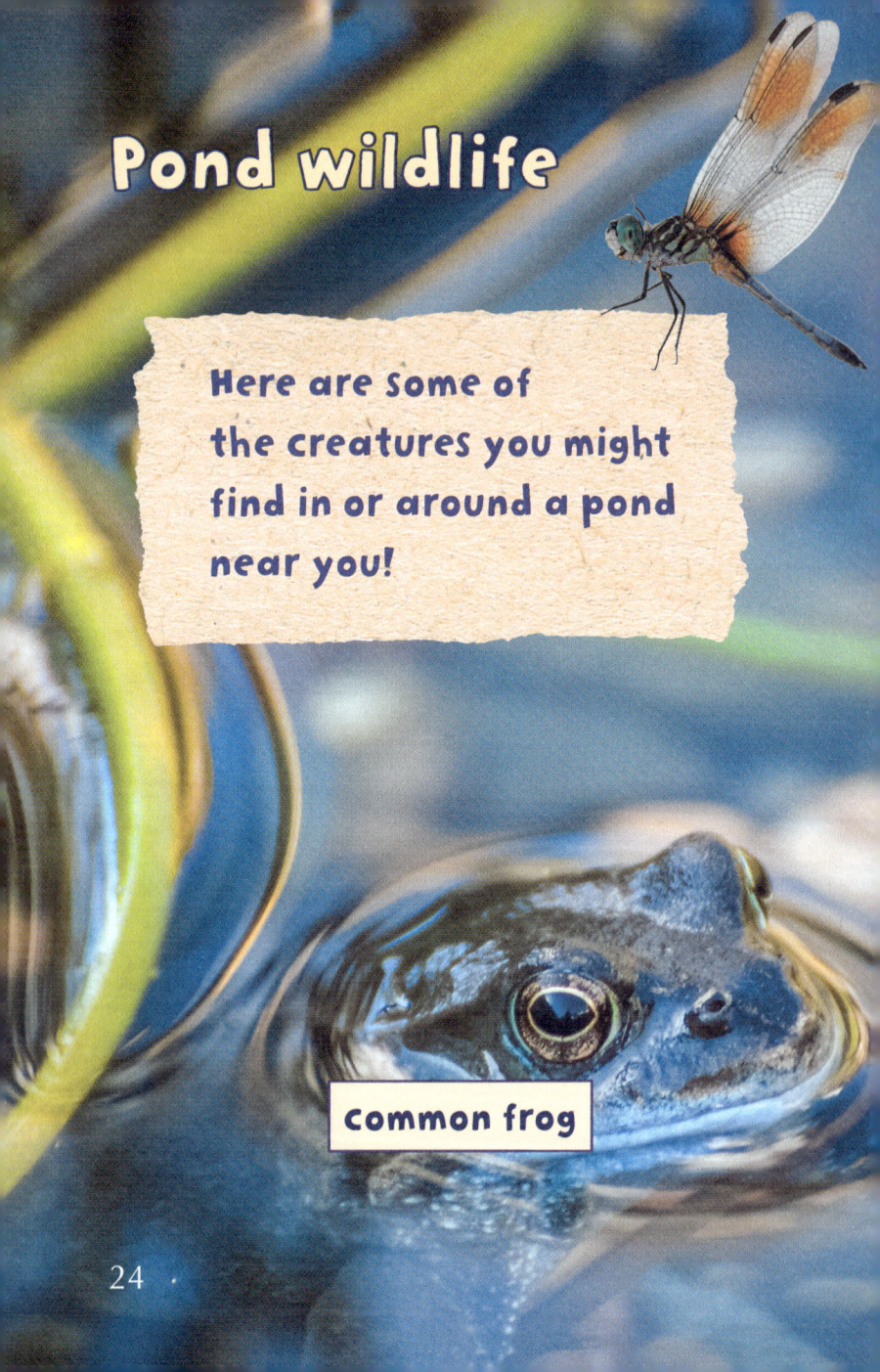

Here are some of the creatures you might find in or around a pond near you!

Common frog

dragonfly

water snail

pond skater

smooth newt

Chapter 3

Ash and Grandma take a well-earned slice of cake and some fresh masala tea. "Your grandfather loved gardening," says Grandma. "After he passed away, I didn't know what to do, so I just covered it all up. He would love what we are doing here: what *you* are doing, Ash. He would be so proud." Ash feels as tall as a tree – he feels like a hero. He starts flicking through his gardening book and making notes and drawing pictures.

Before Grandma's tea is drunk, Ash has sketched a garden design, and it looks incredible.

There are arches and bug hotels, little fruit trees and a vegetable patch.
"Do you think we can make it like this?" asks Ash. Grandma looks at the design and tears start to jewel in her eyes.

"I'm sorry, Grandma," says Ash seriously. "We don't have to do any of it if you don't like it."

Grandma sweeps Ash up in
a massive hug. "Don't like it?
Don't like it? Ash, I love it! We will
make it look exactly like this, but we'll
have to do it slowly. A lot of this we can
do ourselves, but we will need to shop
for some materials. We will have to save
and do it bit by bit."

Ash's head starts to overflow with ideas.
"That's okay, Grandma, I know some of
our friends will help out. I'll save all my
pocket money until we have enough to
get everything we need."

Grandma smiles like a sunrise.
"Oh, I can think of a few ways that we
can raise some money for the garden,"
she says.

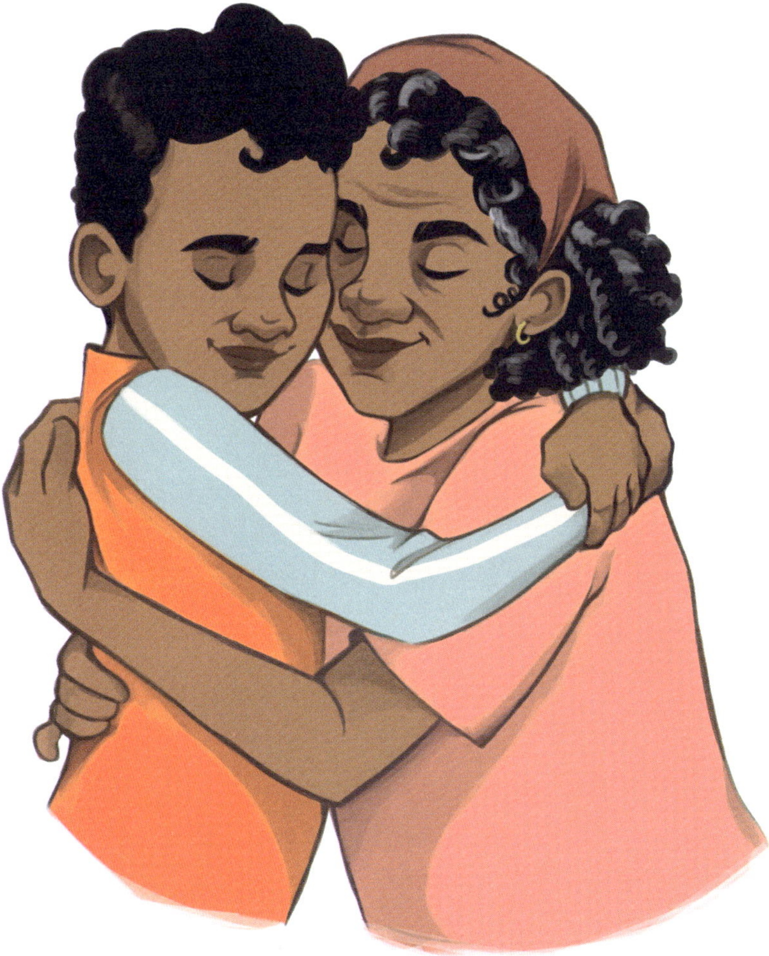

Grandma and Ash go to the supermarket. "Remember, Ash," says Grandma, "you have to spend money to make money." They put bags and bags of flour, boxes and boxes of eggs, packets of butter and mountains of sugar into their trolley, along with almost a tree-load of lemons.

"What will we do with all these, Grandma?" Ash asks curiously.

"You'll see!" says Grandma.

Back at home, Grandma asks Ash to butter the cupcake trays. Grandma has lots and lots of cupcake trays. "These are from my bakery days – that's where I met your grandfather. He came into my bakery one day and we chatted and laughed. From that time on he had me laughing every day."

After a day of weighing, mixing, folding, grating, baking and icing, Ash and Grandma have made over 200 cupcakes! The kitchen is full, every surface piled high with cooling lemon drizzle cupcakes.

Grandma takes out a notepad and paper and starts calculating. She writes down numbers and crosses them out until ... "That will do it, I guess!" she says. "We need to sell 150 of these cupcakes for £1.50 each. Then we'll have more than enough to get everything we need to finish the garden. What's more, that means we can actually eat some of the cupcakes ourselves!"

Grandma gives Ash a cupcake and he bites into it at once. It is sweet and fluffy and has a gooey lemon curd filling. It tastes like summer has arrived in his mouth, warm, sweet and bright.

"But where will we sell them?" asks Ash.

"Right by the garden," replies Grandma. "We'll hang up your design and show everyone what we are trying to achieve."

Garden design

Garden designers plot out how gardens will look using plans like this.

Make your own plan.
Use A4 squared paper.

Draw a map. Add in flower beds and vegetable patches.

patio

pond

Where will the paths go?

big tree

vegetables

What features will you add?

Chapter 4

Next morning, Ash is up with the sun. His whole being is fizzing with the excitement of selling cupcakes! He can't wait to make enough money to get everything they need to finish the garden.

The first few drops of rain splash down on the table Grandma has put outside for the cupcake stand. "Just a few drops!" says Grandma. "It looks like it is stopping before it even starts. We'll keep the cakes inside for now."

The raindrops soak into the copy of Ash's design that they've stuck up on the garden fence. "We'll take this down for now, just until the shower passes," says Grandma.

The next cascade of drops has Ash and Grandma running inside. The sky becomes a tempestuous soup of black and grey. There are furious flashes of lightning, and rumbling, roaring, rattles of thunder.

The storm is so serious that it even gets its own name: Bertha. Pictures of fallen trees and burst riverbanks flash across the TV screen. But none of the TV channels have noticed the damage done to Ash's garden. It is a muddy bog covered in twigs and leaves, because branches have fallen from the surrounding trees. The seedlings have washed away, and the fence … the entire fence has gone, stolen by the wind!

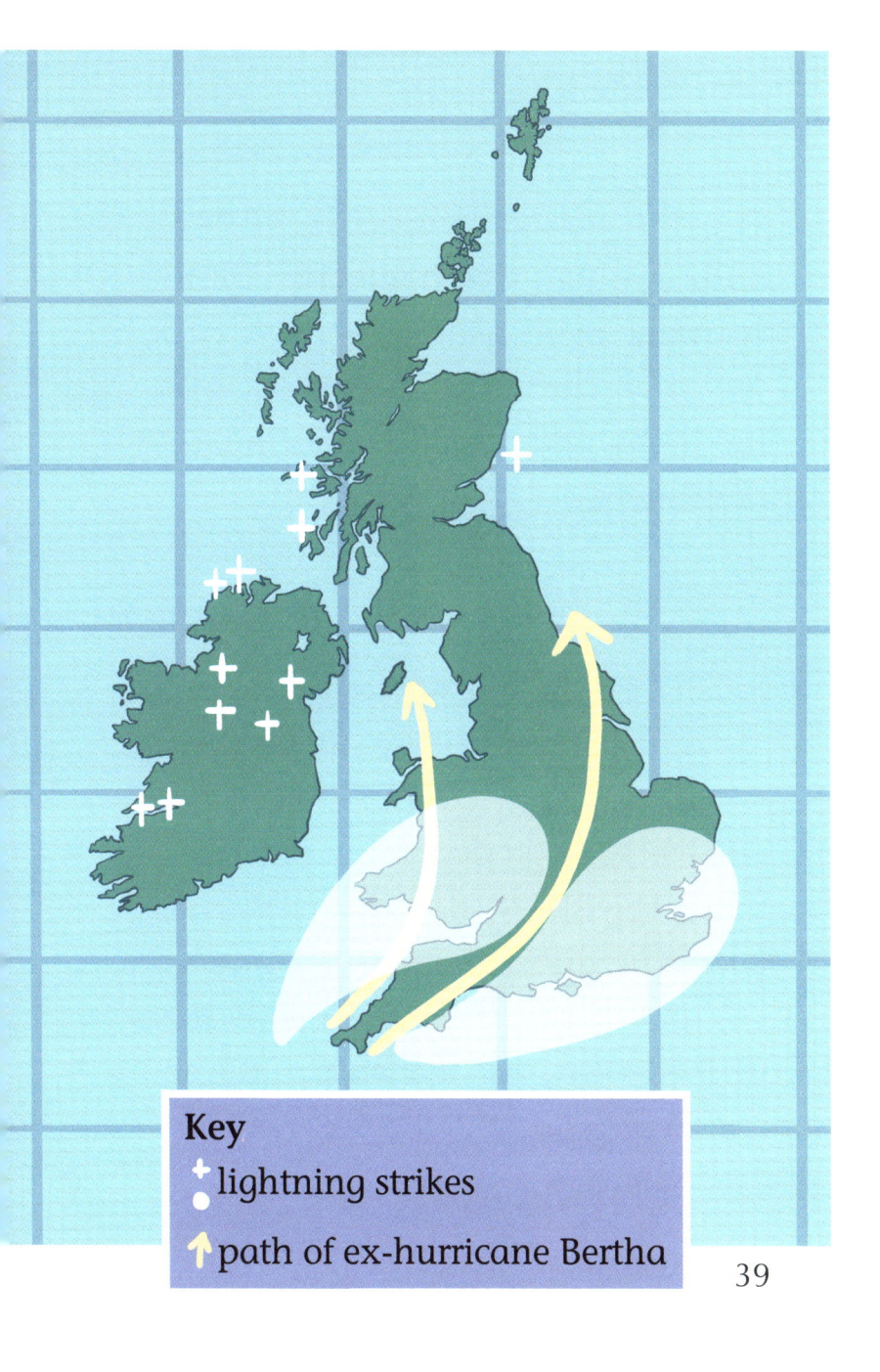

Key
✚ lightning strikes
●
↑ path of ex-hurricane Bertha

39

Over the next couple of days the storm dies down, but it continues to rain. The pond overflows, and some of the pond plants float up and out onto the boggy ground. Ash can't stand seeing the garden like this! He wants to get out there and sort it all out, but he would probably just get stuck in the soggy mud.

Grandma tries to cheer Ash up, as it rains for hours on end. They play board games, read magazines, watch films and even replant some of their house plants. But nothing seems to get Ash out of the mood he's in until Grandma fishes out some old photo albums.

There are photos of Grandma and Grandad when they were young, visiting gardens all over the world. "Wherever we went, your grandfather would want to visit the local botanical gardens. It was never really my thing, but it would soothe him. Now I realise I've missed it. I have missed the flowers and the leaves and the branches in the trees. I have missed the buzzing of bees and the swoop and dive of swifts and swallows rushing to scoop up insects. I've missed all those things almost as much as I have missed your grandfather."

After three days of wind and rain Ash and Grandma find that they are greeted with glorious sunshine – and a garden that looks like it's been trashed by a giant.

"What will we do about
the missing fences?" asks Ash.
Grandma looks out at the garden that
has now merged into the fields and
forest beyond.

"Maybe we should leave them," says Grandma. For the first time Ash notices how the garden is not just one place, how it doesn't end where the fence ends. It's part of the fields and forests beyond, and the land beyond that, and the seas and mountains beyond that.

"Can we do that?" asks Ash. "Can we just leave the fences down?"

Grandma breathes deeply, and smiles. "I don't see why not".

Storm Bertha

On Sunday 10th August 2014, a massive storm hit the UK! It was actually the very end of a hurricane — so its official name was Ex-hurricane Bertha.

cars stuck in water, Cardiff, Wales

massive waves in Wales!

The storm did a lot of damage. Some places got twice the average rainfall for the whole of August — in just one day!

Chapter 5

The following day, the sun continues to shine, and the garden dries out. Slowly but surely Ash and Grandma start to return it to what it was before the storm. They start by putting out their stall and a fresh batch of cakes to sell.

Everyone in the village comes by, and some come more than once. But they don't only visit for cakes – they also come to drop things off.

Mrs Wilson from down the road brings onion plants. "These grow huge!" she says.

Maria, who lives above the post office, comes with a bird box. "Make sure you face it north-east, so it doesn't get too much sun," she says, curling a finger around one of her locs.

Carl the mechanic comes over with three large tyres from the garage. "You can stack these and plant potatoes in them," he says. They are big enough for Ash to stand in!

fill a tyre with soil

stack another tyre on top and fill that with soil

plant potatoes

wait for them to grow – then enjoy!

At the end of the day, Grandma counts up the money from the cupcake sale. All but one of the cakes have been sold, leaving one for Grandma and Ash to share while they start to plan their trip to get some lovely things for the garden. This time, not from the garden centre but from a garden fair.

The garden fair only happens once a year in their local town. It is huge! There are tree ferns and palms, and citrus trees for growing in conservatories and large greenhouses. There are also workshops showing people how to plant various things from bulbs to roses to bushes. But Ash knows what he wants. He takes Grandma's hand and leads her to the fruit trees.

There are lots of small fruit trees
in pots, perfect for smaller spaces.
"Oh look, Ash, a Bramley apple tree!
Perfect for desserts! Your grandfather
loved a good apple crumble,"
says Grandma.

The seller comes over and starts telling
them about all the different varieties of
apple and pear, plum and cherry trees.
She shows them how you can take
a branch from one tree and attach it
to another.

"It's called grafting," says the seller.
"We take a shoot from one tree, and
graft it on to another tree, to get a tree
with the qualities we want.

fruit variety

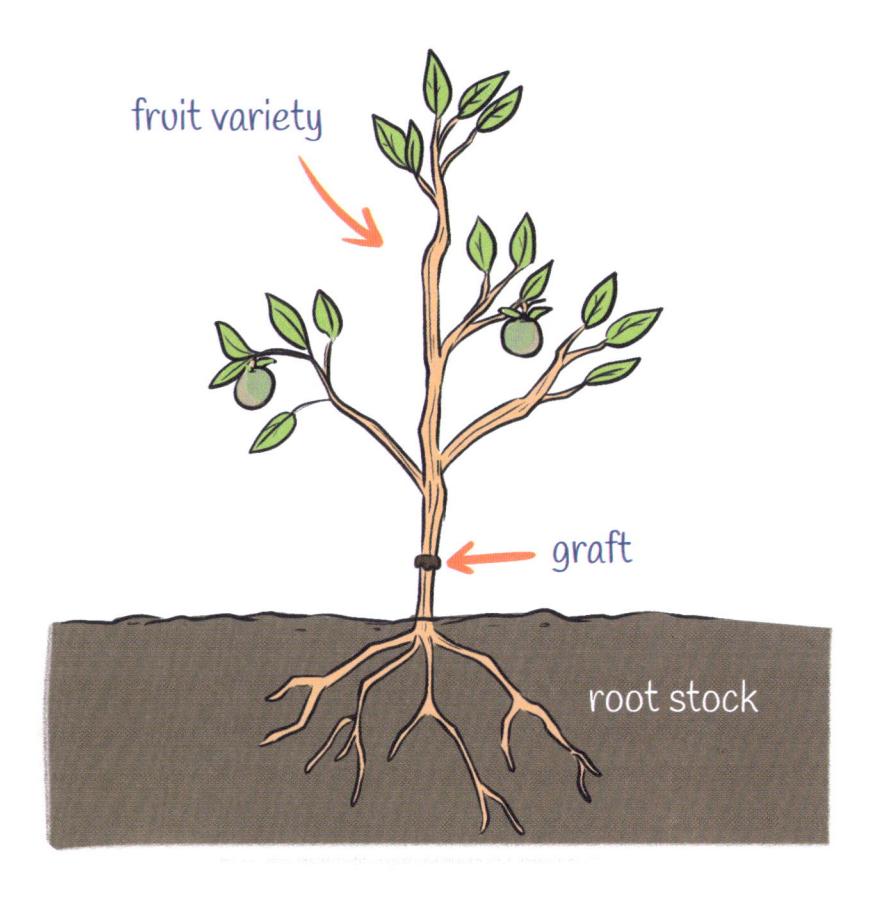

graft

root stock

We can take a shoot from a tall tree with delicious fruit, and graft it on to the roots of a small tree. Then we get a short tree with delicious fruit!" Ash's eyes become as wide as apples with amazement.

Next they stop by a stall filled with seeds – every kind of seed you could think of. There are pumpkin seeds, cauliflower seeds and courgette seeds, tomato seeds and even cucumber seeds. "These will do for our vegetable patch," says Ash.

They get busy picking out seeds of different sorts and even find some seed potatoes. "We can plant these in the tyres Carl gave us," says Ash.

By the end of the day, they have some fruit trees, a garden arch, some seating and many packets of seeds. "The garden is going to look brilliant!" says Ash, before he nods off on the drive back home.

Vegetable patch

If you've planted vegetables, you need to know how to look after them! Here's how to keep them healthy.

Tomato plants need plenty of water and plant food, and to be protected from the cold. Plant outside in May to avoid frost.

Potatoes grow under these shoots! Heap up soil around them as they grow, to help the potatoes to form underground.

The round green thing under the yellow flower is a tiny pumpkin. They need a lot of water and plant food to grow big.

This will grow into a big cauliflower. Water it and cover with a net to keep it safe from insects like caterpillars.

Chapter 6

The following days are busy. Ash is up early with Grandma each day – planting trees, removing weeds, planting seeds, and building the seating and the arch. Finally, after a lot of hard work, the garden is finished.

Ash frowns. "What if the plants die? What if no wildlife finds our pond?" Grandma says, "We just have to be patient."

Every day Ash checks on the garden. He checks for frogs in the pond – there are none.

He checks for birds in the bird box – there are none.

He checks for seedlings in the veg patch – there are none.

As the days roll by with no change, Ash feels his heart sink. He stops checking on the garden, leaving Grandma to water it alone.

But one day Grandma wakes
Ash up early. "I want to stay in
bed, Grandma!" he says rubbing sleep
from his eyes and feeling as low as
a sodden, mouldy old log.

"Hurry up, because I have something
to show you," says Grandma. She leads
him downstairs, through the kitchen
and down the short hallway that leads
to the garden.

Ash hasn't been out here for ages. The memory of his disappointment about nothing growing makes his heart sink even lower. But when Grandma opens the garden door, Ash sees a riot of foliage! There are insects buzzing and birds swooping.

The veg patch is filled with lots of tiny little plants, and even some weeds. "We'll need to get those out," says Grandma.

Ash spies a robin with a beak full of twigs flying in and out of the bird box. "It looks like we've got a new guest!" says Grandma.

In the pond, Ash spies …
"A frog, Grandma! A frog has found our pond."

Ash and Grandma spend the rest of the day removing weeds, tidying the garden, sharing news and watering all the plants. By the edges of the garden where the fence used to be, Ash notices that some of the flowers from the forest and fields beyond have made their way into the garden.

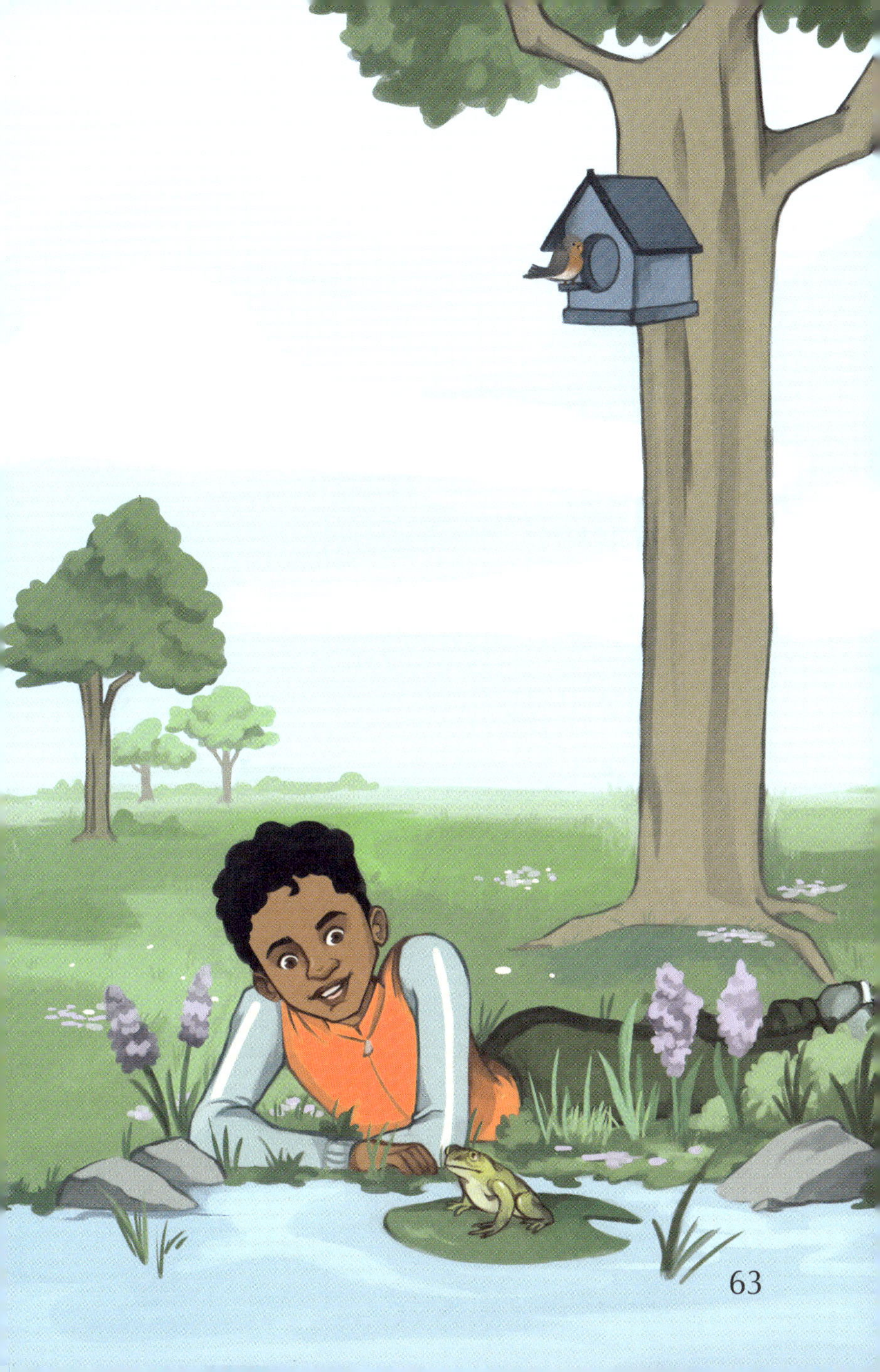

He watches as a huge bumble bee
flies lazily into the garden, lands on
a daffodil, and slowly flies out again.
Ash breathes in a deep breath that feels
as wide as the horizon.

The sun shines all day and they eat
lunch and dinner in the garden, staying
to watch the sunset. Just as they get
ready to go inside, something starts
to rise from the pond, a-flittering and
a-fluttering, a-gathering and a-dancing.

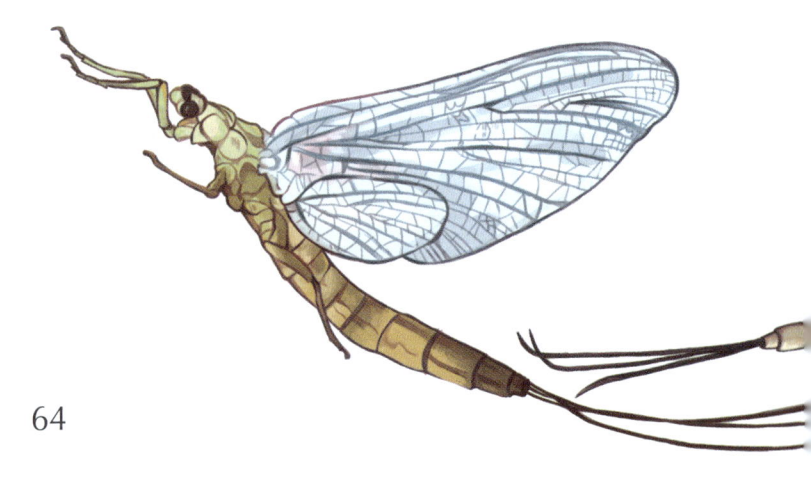

"Mayflies!" cries Grandma, as hundreds of beautiful mayflies swoop and dive up into the air. They form a silhouette sky dance for Ash and Grandma to gasp at. For a moment the flies come together and for a single second Grandma and Ash are wide-eyed as they seem to take the shape of a man! It's a man who looks like Grandad, right down to the cap he always wore. Then the flies scatter towards the setting sun, with light glinting off their silvery wings.

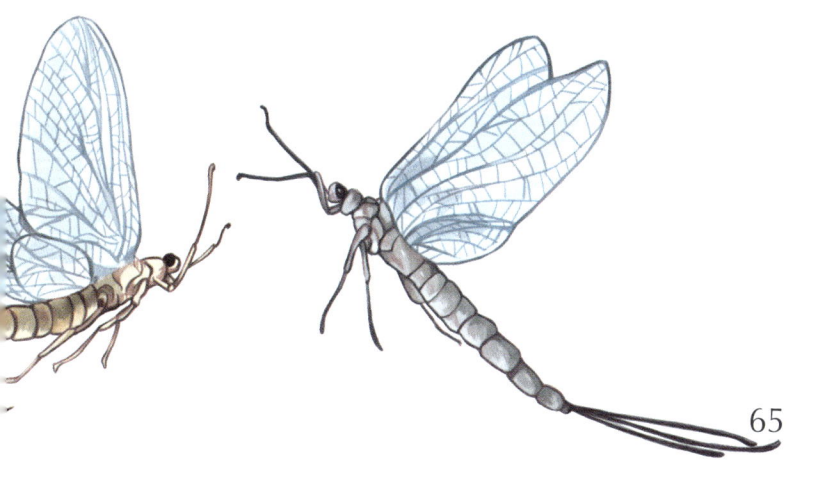

In the days and weeks that follow, Ash and Grandma see no end of visitors to their garden. People bring chairs and blankets, cakes and curries, sandwiches, pickles and jams, guitars and tambourines. Soon Ash can't tell where the garden ends and the horizon begins. It all stretches out ahead of him and Grandma and everyone, and they all enjoy it together.

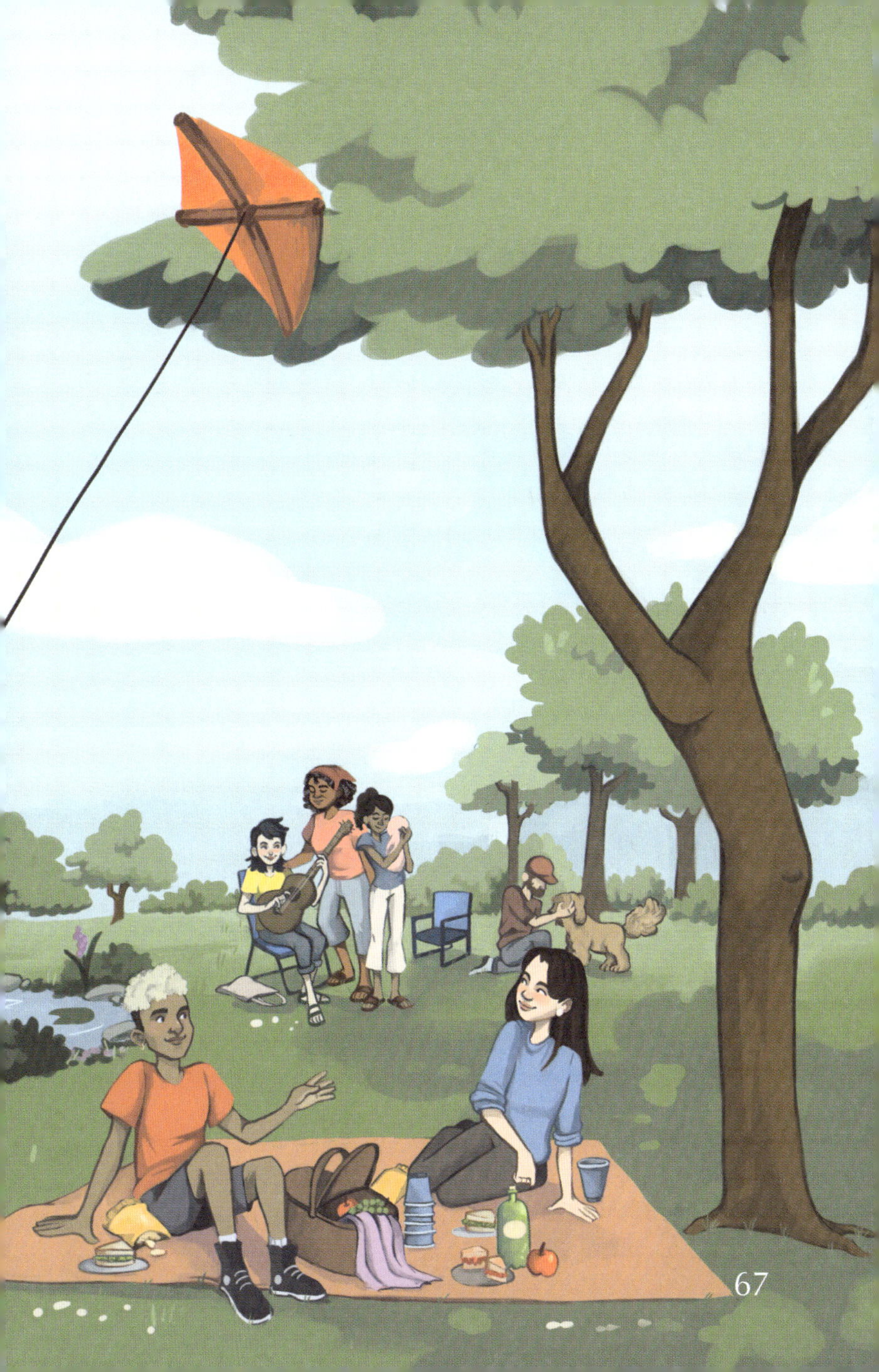

Mayfly life cycle

Mayflies live for about one day in their final, winged form. They spend most of their lives underwater.

Adult mayflies lay their eggs in water.

Mayflies swarm and mate.

The eggs hatch. The babies are called nymphs.

Fully grown nymphs shed their skins and turn into a winged fly called a sub-imago.

After a few hours, they change again! They burst their skins again and out comes the adult mayfly.

About the author

How did you get into writing?
It all started when the wonderful Jean Binta Breeze visited my school and read a poem. From that moment on I felt that poetry and writing was something I could take part in.

Joseph Coelho

What do you hope readers will get out of the book?
I hope that readers start to take an interest in plants and growing them either in a garden, on a balcony or on a windowsill. There is something incredibly satisfying about growing a seedling into a fully grown plant.

Does anything in this book relate to your experiences?
I have always enjoyed growing things and am very lucky to have a garden where I grow lots of vegetables. But before that, I had an allotment and loved swapping seeds and vegetables with the other allotment users.

Why did you want to write this book?
I wanted to share my passion for gardening, and honour the work it takes to make a garden flourish and how rewarding it is.

What is it like for you to write?
It's a wonder and a joy. I get to create, invent and share new worlds and characters. I also get to explore my feelings, and let people know that someone else has, at one point or another, felt exactly the way they feel.

Do you have a garden? If so, what's it like?
I do – it has a pond filled with wildlife, a big wooden arch in the middle and lots of beds where I grow vegetables. I also have several fruit trees.

What would be your top tip for helping wildlife?
Build a pond! Lots of ponds have been lost over the years. All life depends on water, so creating a pond will encourage all sorts of creatures to visit your garden. If you don't have a garden, a dish of water on a windowsill for birds is a help.

What would your dream garden be like?
It would be huge, with fully-grown trees. I would have a tree house and a massive pond that I could swim in! I should make a start on that now!

About the illustrator

What made you want to be an illustrator?

I think in everything that I've ever tried I always came back to illustrating, I think the answer is just that simple I loved art so I pursued illustrating.

How did you get into illustration? Monique Steele

I have always loved drawing. Growing up my mum would buy me tracing paper for me because I would always try to copy the illustrations in my storybooks. I think my love for reading fostered my love for drawing because I would see the beautiful illustrations and want to recreate them Then, eventually, I started trying to draw my own characters.

What was the most difficult thing about illustrating this book?

My most challenging illustration was definitely the dreary garden after the storm. It was difficult getting the colours to look nice while showing how gloomy and muddy everything was.

What did you like best about illustrating this book?
I really loved getting a chance to draw things I don't usually get to draw like newts and frogs and mayflies!

Is there anything in this book that relates to your own experiences?
My maternal side of the family are all avid gardeners. So, Ash's experience making a garden with his grandmother reminded me of my family creating their own gardens full of flowers and fruit trees and vegetables.

How do you bring a character to life in an illustration?
I always focus on the character's personality first and how to get that to shine through in a drawing. Asking myself questions like: "What would Ash's grandmother wear to start a gardening project?" helps me piece together what this character would be like if they were real.

Do you have a garden? If so, what's it like?
I don't have my own garden, unfortunately. I wasn't blessed with green fingers, but I sometimes help my Mum when she gardens. She's a big fan of orchids so you can see many of those in her garden as well as some fruit trees like banana and mango trees.

Book chat

What have you learned from reading this book?

What was the most interesting part of the book?

Have you ever done any gardening? What did you do?

If you had to give the book a new title, what would you choose?

Which part of the book did you like best, and why?

Did this book remind you of anything you have experienced in real life?

If you could ask the author anything, what would it be?

Have you ever seen any of the animals or plants mentioned in the book?

Book challenge:

Design your dream garden.

Collins BIG CAT

Published by Collins
An imprint of HarperCollins*Publishers*

The News Building
1 London Bridge Street
London SE1 9GF
UK

Macken House
39/40 Mayor Street Upper
Dublin 1
D01 C9W8
Ireland

Text © Joseph Coelho 2023
Design and illustrations ©
HarperCollins*Publishers* Limited 2023

10 9 8 7 6 5 4 3 2 1

ISBN 978-0-00-862459-0

All rights reserved. No part of this publication may be reproduced, stored in a retrieval system, or transmitted in any form by any means, electronic, mechanical, photocopying, recording or otherwise, without the prior written permission of the Publisher or a licence permitting restricted copying in the United Kingdom issued by the Copyright Licensing Agency Ltd, 5th Floor, Shackleton House, 4 Battle Bridge Lane, London SE1 2HX.

British Library Cataloguing-in-Publication Data
A catalogue record for this publication is available from the British Library.

Download the teaching notes and word cards to accompany this book at:
http://littlewandle.org.uk/signupfluency/

Get the latest Collins Big Cat news at
collins.co.uk/collinsbigcat

Author: Joseph Coelho
Illustrator: Monique Steele (Illo Agency)
Publisher: Lizzie Catford
Product manager and
  commissioning editor: Caroline Green
Series editor: Charlotte Raby
Development editor: Catherine Baker
Project manager: Emily Hooton
Content editor: Daniela Mora Chavarría
Phonics reviewer: Rachel Russ
Proofreader: Gaynor Spry
Cover designer: Sarah Finan
Typesetter: 2Hoots Publishing Services Ltd
Production controller: Katharine Willard

Collins would like to thank the teachers and children at the following schools who took part in the trialling of Big Cat for Little Wandle Fluency: Burley And Woodhead Church of England Primary School; Chesterton Primary School; Lady Margaret Primary School; Little Sutton Primary School; Parsloes Primary School.

Printed and bound in the UK using 100% Renewable Electricity at Martins the Printers Ltd

MIX
Paper | Supporting responsible forestry
FSC™ C007454

This book is produced from independently certified FSC™ paper to ensure responsible forest management.

For more information visit:
www.harpercollins.co.uk/green

Acknowledgements
The publishers gratefully acknowledge the permission granted to reproduce the copyright material in this book. Every effort has been made to trace copyright holders and to obtain their permission for the use of copyright material. The publishers will gladly receive any information enabling them to rectify any error or omission at the first opportunity.

p12, p24t, p34, p46t, p47b, p56t, p68t Only background/Shutterstock, pp12–13 iMarzi/Shutterstock, pp24–25 David Ridley/Shutterstock, p24tr & p25l Le Do/Shutterstock, p25tr Eric Isselee/Shutterstock, p25cl Zadiraka Evgenii/Shutterstock, p25b Squeeb Creative/Shutterstock, pp34–35 p-jitti/Shutterstock, pp46–47 Robert Smith/Alamy Live News/Alamy Stock Photo, p46 Polly Thomas/Alamy Stock Photo, p47 atgof.co/Alamy Stock Photo, p56 Kleo foto/Shutterstock, pp56–57 amenic181/Shutterstock, p57t Jozef Sowa/Shutterstock, p57c M.Gunsyah/Shutterstock, p57b Angel DiBilio/Shutterstock, pp68–69 Rich Carey/Shutterstock, p68c blickwinkel/Alamy Stock Photo, p68b Mladen Mitrinovic/Shutterstock, p69t tartmany/Shutterstock, p69c Ingo Arndt/Nature Picture Library, p69b bt_photo/Shutterstock.